Safer Income for Life®

SAFER INCOME FOR LIFE®
Retirement Mistakes That Could Cost You Hundreds of Thousands of Dollars
Copyright © 2022 Charles and David Bartman
All rights reserved.
ISBN: 978-1-956220-18-6

Text formatting and composition by Emily Fritz

Disclaimer
Senior Financial Center, Inc. and the authors are not endorsed by the Social Security Administration or any other government agency. The content of this publication is the opinion of Senior Financial Center Inc. and the authors and is intended for basic informational purposes only, subject to the authors' professional limitations. It should be understood that Senior Financial Center, Inc., the authors, and the publisher are not engaged in rendering legal, accounting, or other financial services through this medium. Senior Financial Center, Inc., the authors, and the publisher shall not be liable for your misuse of this material and shall have neither liability nor responsibility to anyone with respect to any loss or damage caused, or alleged to be caused, directly or indirectly by the information contained in this book. Senior Financial Center, Inc., the authors, and the publisher do not guarantee that anyone following these strategies, suggestions, tips, ideas, or techniques will become successful. If legal advice or other expert assistance is required, the services of a competent professional should be sought.

All rights reserved. No portion of this book may be reproduced mechanically, electronically, or by any other means, including photocopying, without written permission of the author. It is illegal to copy the book, post it to a website, or distribute it by any other means without permission from the authors.

Safer Income for Life®
Retirement Mistakes That Could Cost You
Hundreds of Thousands of Dollars

Charles and David Bartman

Contents

Preface 1
Introduction 5
1: Guaranteed Money 7
2: Rule of 100 17
3: Qualified, Non-Qualified, and Roth Accounts . 23
4: Required Minimum Distribution
and the SECURE Act 33
5: Social Security Secrets 41
6: How Social Security Rules Affect You 57
7: Free Social Security Optimization 69
8: It May Be Possible to Avoid Hundreds
of Thousands of Dollars in Taxes 75
9: Mistakes to Avoid if You're In or
Near Retirement 83
10: Are Annuities Safe, Guaranteed,
and Insured? 103
11: Annuity Myths, Pros, and Cons 111
12: Understanding Annuities 121
Conclusion 129
Glossary 135
About the Authors 143

Preface

Senior Financial Center, Inc. offers complimentary Social Security optimization classes to the public because of a situation I found myself in when I was nearing age sixty-two. I had no clue whether I should claim my Social Security benefits at age sixty-two or wait and claim later. I decided to call other advisors and radio show hosts, locally and around the country, to get their opinions. I was surprised at the two answers I got to my question: (1) collect the benefits at age sixty-two to invest in the market and (2) call Social Security for answers.

Why in the world would anyone want to put their Social Security money in the stock market? If you had a pension, would you take your pension and invest it in the stock market? The second answer is just as bad. I called Social Security three times, asking the same question, and I got three different answers.

I ended up performing my own due diligence and searched for someone who would run a Social Security optimization analysis for my wife and me. The optimization analysis showed us four different strategies that were available to us to collect a combined benefit over our life expectancy of more than $1.2 million.

I filed for spousal benefits at age sixty-six years and six months, not knowing I was eligible to collect spousal benefits at age sixty-six. Because I didn't collect at age sixty-six, I was retroactively paid $750 a month for the previous six months and received a check for $4,500. I then continued to collect $750 a month until I turned seventy years old for a total of $36,000.

I didn't even know I was entitled to spousal benefits—and that it wouldn't change my wife's benefit at all. I then switched to my own benefit, which increased my benefits by 57 percent, plus the cost-of-living adjustment (COLA) increased our benefits by 13.6 percent since 2017. In the state of Michigan, there is no state tax on Social Security benefits.

Preface

Without the optimization analysis and the specific instructions to take to the Social Security Administration on *how* and *when* to file, I would not have known what to do. The report cost me $149, but when I found out how much I was missing out on, I felt that was a good return on my investment. I couldn't write out that check fast enough!

This is exactly why my son David and I wrote this book. Social Security will be one of the most important decisions you'll make, along with tax planning, at a time when you'll need the money the most—in your retirement.

— **Charles Bartman**

Introduction

Do you have enough money to retire? Planning for your retirement should be at the top of your list of priorities, especially if you're in or near retirement. Investment mistakes made during your sequence of return (the volatility of the market) could have you running out of money. You should be enjoying yourself in retirement, not worrying if you have enough money to get you through it.

Age should make a difference in your risk tolerance, but it's never too early or too late to educate yourself about the decisions you'll need to make to plan for income, safety, and growth in retirement. The sooner the better; you don't want to be rushed into making critical decisions just a few months before you decide to retire.

CHAPTER ONE
Guaranteed Money

Running out of money is worse than death.

—Carole Fleck, AARP

If your retirement assets are in equities or variable investments such as stocks, bonds, real estate investment trusts, mutual funds, variable annuities, and precious metals such as gold, then they are all subject to market volatility within their asset classes. This is what we call the *maybe money* (market risk) portion of your portfolio: *Maybe you'll make money, maybe you won't.* There are no guarantees. When you retire, will your money be there when you need it the most?

If you mention to your advisor that you're concerned about a market correction and losing money, the first thing they'll probably want to do is set up a meeting to go over your financial situation. They'll recommend reallocating your assets to diversify into more conservative investments that may help preserve your assets from market volatility. We like to use a gambling analogy for this advice: You might as well walk into a casino and say, "I'm going to diversify—a little poker, some blackjack, and then on to the slot machines." Even if your money is invested conservatively in equities or variable investments and the market declines, then *all* your money is still at risk from market volatility, and it's still possible to lose money.

Obviously, it's your money, so you have to feel comfortable in how your hard-earned dollars are invested, but at least some of it needs to be safe and able to generate an income in retirement. Prepare yourself for the day you retire; you don't want to outlive your money. That's why it's so important to consider how much money you'll need in retirement. What are your plans once you stop working? Will you need to pay for medical insurance? Will you need long-term care? How will inflation and taxes affect your retirement?

Whether you're already retired or planning your retirement, you should think seriously about being in preservation mode, protecting what you've acquired for retirement. If you have most or all your money at risk in the market, where's your safe money? You've worked far too long and hard to attempt a home run in the ninth inning of the baseball game. You can't risk striking out with your retirement savings when you're in or near retirement, hoping that the stock market cooperates with you. You must use safe-money alternatives to diversify as a way to provide a lifetime of income for you and your spouse, rather than losing your retirement assets from a market decline.

You cannot afford to have the majority of your money in equities when dealing with a declining market. This could devastate your plans for retirement and cause you to run out of money. If you lose 50 percent of your investments in a market decline, you would need a 100 percent gain just to break even. It would take you quite a while to get back to where you were.

Has your advisor put most of your assets in conservative equities and very little in cash? You should be wondering why. Do you think it may be because the advisor is more concerned about being on your payroll and collecting a fee than on you outliving your money in retirement? Ask yourself, what's the agenda if your advisor keeps most of your hard-earned money in the market? Obviously, your advisor gets paid whether you make money or not, if your money is at risk in the market. If your advisor moves any portion of your investments to cash or money market accounts for safety, there are no fees to collect.

Why wouldn't you consider an income for life that's guaranteed and insured? Are you aware that no commissions or fees are taken out of a guaranteed money account to pay an advisor? And unlike equities or variable investments in the market, a guaranteed money account doesn't lose money from a market decline.

Think seriously about protecting your principal with guaranteed money to generate a lifetime income stream. As a portion of your portfolio, guaranteed money is designed to last you throughout your retirement years.

In the past, many Ford and General Motors employees converted their lump-sum buyouts into their own personal pensions. While they withdraw income from their pension, the lump sum continues to make money if the market goes up. If the market goes down, there is no loss of principal, and they still have their personal pension to collect on a single or joint payout until the day they pass away. If they had opted for the company pension, the lump sum would have stayed with the company. Why would anyone give up the lump sum?

Let's look at some safe-money alternatives.

Banks and Credit Unions

The Federal Deposit Insurance Corporation guarantees your bank deposit. The National Credit Union Administration guarantees credit unions. These types of financial institutions offer fixed interest rates on savings and certificates of deposit (CDs), but a withdrawal from your CD prior to its maturity date can result in a penalty if you don't adhere to the guidelines.

The interest rates on CDs and savings accounts are very low. Because of the low interest rates, you as an investor could be exposed to the risk of inflation. For example, say the bank or credit union offered a twelve-month CD for 0.70 percent. The Rule of 72 says to take 72 and divide it by the interest rate, which tells you how long it would take you to double your money. With a rate of 0.70 percent, it would take you approximately 103 years to double your money.

Obviously, none of us are planning on living that long. The whopping one-tenth of 0.01 percent on savings accounts would take you 720 years to double your investment. So who's being taken advantage of here? It's clearly the person with a CD or savings account, along with the person applying for a credit card with interest rates in the double digits.

It's not the responsibility of the bank or credit union to help you keep up with inflation. They couldn't care less if you're getting a negative return with inflation on your deposit. A good place to learn about the most recent bank rates in the United States is the Bankrate website at: http://www.Bankrate.com.

United States Treasury Securities

When you purchase United States Treasury securities, you presumably minimize any default. However, these guaranteed investments can also have a very low yield, whether it's yield to maturity or yield to call. The United States

Department of the Treasury issues these government debt instruments to finance the national debt of the United States.

Generally speaking, there are four types of marketable US treasuries: T-bills, T-notes, T-bonds, and Treasury inflation-protected securities, which are often referred to simply as Treasurys. Since 2012, the management of government debt has been arranged by the Bureau of the Fiscal Service, succeeding the Bureau of the Public Debt. Many of these securities can be purchased directly from the US Treasury on their website at: TreasuryDirect.gov.

Fixed and Fixed-Indexed Annuities (FIAs)

The United States experienced a devastating recession from September 2007 to June 2009. Retirement accounts were decimated to the tune of $2.4 trillion. That's right—not millions or billions but trillions. If investors had used fixed or (FIAs) with a portion of their portfolios, they would have had the following advantages:

- No loss of principal from market declines
- Growth potential that can be tax-deferred

- Allocation options to participate in market-linked indexes with market-type returns
- Guaranteed and insured
- Various choices for crediting methods
- Income flexibility
- Optional rider for a lifetime of income
- Optional long-term care
- Optional enhanced death benefit
- Probate avoidance

Annuity contracts are not invested in an index. You are paid off the performance of an index. If the index is rising, you make money. If the index is declining, you won't lose a dime of your principal from the volatility of the market. Obviously, you can't say the same for your investments in the market.

History of Annuities

Domitius Ulpian is credited with being the world's first annuity dealer in ancient Rome, circa AD 211. Annuities date back to the Roman era. They were issued to soldiers as a way of thanking them for their loyal service.

Benjamin Franklin supported the concept of annuities, and when he passed away on April

17, 1790, his will left annuities to the cities of Philadelphia and Boston. Boston owned the annuity for over two hundred years, until 1993, when Boston city officials voted to take the lump-sum cash payment. If our research is correct, Philadelphia still owns its annuity to this day.

Civil War soldiers were given annuities instead of land. Prior to his death, President Lincoln supported this program to assist injured or disabled soldiers. After the Civil War, President Grant's administration withdrew many of the annuities, saying that the benefits outweighed their contributions to the war effort. The former veterans pursued legal action, and a few years later the Supreme Court restored the annuities.

Today, insurance companies and state lotteries issue annuities. At one time, banks were allowed to issue annuities, and many of them offered their own forms of annuities. During the financial turmoil of 1919 and just after the end of World War II, individual states began setting up guidelines that made it illegal for banks to issue annuities unless an insurance company issued the annuity.

Each state now has its own rules, statutes, or administrative codes, with a corresponding administrator or commissioner to help govern the sale of annuities in their state. This type of government oversight helps improve the guidelines and standards of annuity sales in each state. This set the rules for the safety of annuities today.

During the Great Depression, life insurance companies that issued annuities considered their standards safe and secure. People's financial futures were preserved because of the safety that annuities provided during the Great Depression, along with the financial strength and claims-paying ability of the issuing insurance company.

Annuities have survived wars, the Great Depression, and recessions, including the devastating market declines of 2000, 2007–2009, and the COVID-19 crisis. Fixed or fixed-indexed annuities have never lost a dime of investors' principal due to market volatility.

CHAPTER TWO
Rule of 100

I'm more concerned with the return of my money than the return on my money.

—Will Rogers

The "Rule of 100" says you subtract your age from one hundred and invest the remainder in risky equities. The rest should be 100 percent safe. That's what we refer to as *guaranteed money* (safer money) and *maybe money* (market risk). How much of your retirement money is safe? To properly apply the Rule of 100, you need three things: income, safety, and growth.

Guaranteed money will give you all of these.

Using this rule is a simple way to help determine the correct diversification of assets for your retirement. We take into consideration your age, time horizon, liquidity needs, goals, and risk tolerance. Asset diversification in equities does not ensure a better return on your investment and cannot eliminate negative returns from market volatility.

Consider a hypothetical example of the Rule of 100. If you are sixty years old, you should already have 60 percent of your assets in guaranteed money (safer money) and the remaining balance of 40 percent in maybe money (market risk) with no guarantees. As you get older, you should be transferring more of your assets to more conservative assets to preserve what you have and generate an income that will provide for you and your family while avoiding any market corrections.

If you are forty years old, time is on your side and you can take on more risk: 40 percent of your portfolio should be in guaranteed money, and the remaining balance of 60 percent should be in maybe money, the exact opposite of above. This rule of thumb can be used to determine how much risk as an investor you should take at a specific age.

The Rule of 100 employs your present age as a percentage to determine how much of your principal should be used to purchase safe-money alternatives. However, because Americans are living longer, your money has to last longer. You may need the extra growth that equities may or may not provide.

If you're a risk taker, you can adjust the Rule of 100 to add 10 percent more to equities. If you're a conservative investor worried about market declines, subtract 10 percent more from equities. Everyone's situation will vary.

If you're approaching retirement or already retired, you should be looking at preserving what you have to ensure your money will last as long as you do. Know your risk tolerance and adjust your investments to where you're comfortable with the risk versus reward. People will spend more time learning how to program their cell phone, tablet, or computer than they will planning for the most important event in their lives: their retirement. We encourage you to take the time to plan, and as always, we recommend that you consult a financial professional.

Market corrections are inevitable, and many of us have experienced them. For example, during the COVID-19 crisis, the market dropped from a high of 29,551 in February 2020 to a low of 18,591 just a month later in March 2020. That's a 62.97 percent drop that caused the global markets to lose trillions of dollars. Then there was the subprime mortgage collapse that caused the Dow Jones Industrial Average to fall from its high of 14,164 (reached in October 2007) to 6,443 in March 2009. That's a 54 percent plunge in a little under eighteen months, and the real estate bubble burst.

You know how stressful those times were. They were extremely devastating for people already in retirement. This is why we suggest having some of your assets in safe-money alternatives. You don't want to go back to work just to support your lifestyle. If you treat your assets the same way you did when you were employed, it could have a major impact on your retirement.

You need to evaluate your comfort zone. How much risk are you willing to take? An investor's risk tolerance will vary from one person to the next. It's your money, and you've worked hard all your life to accumulate your assets. Many people are uncomfortable talking about their finances, especially during a market correction.

When the markets are in a decline, people have told us that they won't even open their financial statements because they're afraid to see how much money they've lost.

The whole point behind using the Rule of 100 is to consider reallocating some assets into preservation mode as a way of providing income in retirement. We believe this alternative will allow you to sleep a little better at night.

CHAPTER THREE
Qualified, Non-Qualified, and Roth Accounts

Don't save what is left after spending; spend what is left after saving.

—Warren Buffett

Employers set up qualified and non-qualified retirement plans to benefit employees. In 1974, the Employee Retirement Income Security Act defined qualified and non-qualified plans.

The IRS has two ways to treat your money for tax purposes: qualified (pre-tax) and non-qualified (after-tax).

Qualified Accounts

While your money is held in a qualified retirement account, it has the opportunity to grow, tax-deferred, providing you adhere to IRS rules. If you were to withdraw any funds prior to age fifty-nine-and-a-half, you may be penalized 10 percent for early withdrawal, plus taxes would be owed on any qualified money withdrawn.

Qualified accounts were designed to help you save for retirement. Some qualified retirement accounts can include an employer's matching contributions. Tax-deferred retirement plans could include 401(k)s, 403(b)s, 457(b)s, Savings Incentive Match Plan IRAs (SIMPLE IRAs), or Thrift Savings Plans (TSPs).

Some retirement plans, but not all, allow discretionary contributions or nonelective employer contributions. These nonelective contributions made in addition to matching contributions are at the employer's discretion. Such contributions must be paid equally to every employee covered by the plan; they cannot be made only to certain individuals. The employer or an employer profit-sharing plan normally make the matching or discretionary contributions.

Contributions are tax deductible from your taxable income for the year in which they occurred, with the exception of the Roth IRA. However, there are caveats to the maximum annual contribution limits and income limitations with qualified plans. Please consult with a tax or financial professional. Your money can grow tax-deferred, but at some point, you'll have to pay the IRS. If you withdraw money from your qualified plan, you usually create a taxable event, and your taxes will be due for that given tax year.

There are also strict guidelines for withdrawing any funds. You have required minimum distribution (RMD) from your qualified account(s) starting at age seventy-two.

Qualified Account Withdrawals

We have compiled a list of exceptions including RMDs. To avoid the additional 10 percent penalty, we recommend that you consult with a financial or tax professional to follow all current IRS rules and before using the following exceptions or any exception we may have omitted.

You qualify for an exception to the RMD rule if you continue working past the age of seventy-two and are able to delay distributions from your current employer-sponsored retirement plan until you retire. You do not qualify if you own 5 percent or more of a business sponsoring your retirement plan. You also qualify for an exception to the RMD rule if you have distributions to pay for qualified higher education expenses of the taxpayer, the taxpayer's spouse, or any child or grandchild of the taxpayer, at an eligible educational institution for the taxable year.

A series of substantially equal periodic payments, not less frequently than annually, made for the life or life expectancy of the employee or the joint lives of such employees and their designated beneficiaries also qualify you for RMD exceptions. Under this exception, payments must continue for five years or until the taxpayer reaches age fifty-nine-and-a-half, whichever period is longer. If the payments are changed before the end of the required periods for any reason other than the death or disability of the owner, that person will be subject to the 10 percent penalty.

Exceptions also occur in the following situations: (1) distribution to a beneficiary or the estate of an employee on or after the death of the employee, (2) distribution is paid in the case of total or permanent disability and death, (3) funds are received for dividends paid on an employee's securities, and (4) if you are paid under a qualified domestic relation order to an alternate payee.

Two more exceptions relate to medical care: (1) when receiving funds for deductible medical care in excess of 10 percent (7.5 percent for individuals age sixty-five and older) of adjusted gross income (AGI) and (2) when paying for medical insurance without regard to the applicable AGI floor if the individual, including a self-employed individual, has received unemployment compensation under federal or state law for at least twelve weeks and the withdrawal is made in the year such unemployment compensation is received for the following year.

Qualified first-time home-buyer distributions are exceptions, as are payments made after separation from your employer occurring during or after the calendar year you reach the age of fifty-five.

Finally, the funds for qualified reservist distribution made during the period beginning on the date the participant was ordered or called to active duty for a period of at least 180 days, or for an indefinite period as a member of a reserve component, and ending at the close of the active-duty period are considered exceptions.

Converting your qualified retirement accounts to a Roth IRA or cash value life insurance can be tax-free income, if you adhere to IRS guidelines. Tax planning is crucial to avoid unnecessary taxes. You need to consult with a financial professional about converting your qualified retirement accounts to Roth IRAs or cash value life insurance.

Ed Slott, the IRA expert, said, "Life insurance is the only legal way to print money." We've never had anyone complain that their spouse had too much life insurance.

Non-Qualified Accounts

Non-qualified accounts can also be used to convert to tax-free cash value life insurance. Non-qualified plans do not get taxed up front. Taxes are paid before your principal payment is made; the after-tax money invested is called cost basis. The cost basis is not taxable, but the gains over and above the original money invested are.

There is no additional tax advantage when using a non-qualified plan. There's just a difference in when you pay the taxes, which depends on where your non-qualified money is deposited. A 1099-INT form will be issued to the IRS and to you to file your annual tax return on any interest earned over ten dollars. You will require the following information: interest paid on certificates of deposit (CDs); savings at a bank, credit union, or savings institution; bonds using the accrual method; and other forms of taxable interest income such as early withdrawal penalties or federal taxes withheld.

The interest may be taxable that year whether you withdraw money or not. As an investor, you will not pay taxes on non-qualified accounts such as annuities, mutual funds, and stocks until the assets are withdrawn, sold, or dividends are paid rather than paying on an annual basis. An annuity can be a non-qualified retirement plan, which has the tax advantage of deferring your taxes like qualified money.

If you want to protect your money from being taxed every year, purchasing a non-qualified annuity will accomplish that. You will not have to pay taxes on your gains every year, only in a year when you've withdrawn funds from the annuity, but only on the gains. Allowing your money to accumulate faster allows you to pay the taxes when it's convenient for you, not for the IRS.

But there is an exception.

Non-qualified annuities fall under the same IRS rules governing traditional IRAs and other types of retirement plans when it comes to premature distributions. If you withdraw funds prior to age fifty-nine-and-a-half, you may incur a 10 percent penalty plus any taxes owed.

Roth Accounts

William Victor "Bill" Roth Jr. was the legislative sponsor of the individual retirement account plan that bears his name, the Roth IRA. It's been a popular individual retirement account since its introduction under the Taxpayer Relief Act of 1997. The Roth 401(k), which did not become available until 2006, is also named after William Roth Jr.

The status of the Roth IRA sounds like a non-qualified account, but the IRS treats it as a qualified account. To fund a Roth IRA, you use after-tax dollars, with the possibility of having the money grow tax-deferred. On top of that, all your gains are tax-free once your account has been established for five years and you've reached the age of fifty-nine-and-a-half.

For 2022, an individual can contribute annually to both traditional and Roth IRAs, but the amount cannot be more than $6,000 ($7,000 if you're fifty or older). If your annual compensation is less than the annual contribution limit, you cannot exceed that amount for that year. It's a great deal, although there are contribution and income limits.

Before you make any decisions, consult with a financial professional to decide what type of investment meets your specific situation and will meet your investment objectives. Refer to the table below to learn more about Roth IRA income limits.[1]

---

[1] Jean Folger, "Roth and Traditional IRA Contribution Limits for 2021 and 2022," Investopedia.com, March 7, 2022, https://www.investopedia.com/retirement/ira-contribution-limits/

2021 and 2022 Roth IRA Income Limits

Filing Status	2021 Modified AGI	2022 Modified AGI	Contribution Limit
Married filing jointly or qualifying widow(er)	Less than $198,000	Less than $204,000	$6,000 ($7,000 if you're 50 or older)
	$198,000 to $208,000	$204,000 to $214,000	Reduced
	$208,000 or more	$214,000 or more	Not eligible
Single, head of household, or married filing separately (and you didn't live with your spouse at any time during the year)	Less than $125,000	Less than $129,000	$6,000 ($7,000 if you're 50 or older)
	$125,000 to $140,000	$129,000 to $144,000	Reduced
	$140,000 or more	$144,000 or more	Not eligible
Married filing separately (if you lived with your spouse at any time during the year)	Less than $10,000	Less than $10,000	Reduced
	$10,000 or more	$10,000 or more	Not eligible

CHAPTER FOUR
Required Minimum Distribution and the SECURE Act

The question isn't at what age I want to retire, it's at what income.

—George Foreman

Required minimum distribution is the dollar amount the IRS requires to be withdrawn from qualified tax-deferred retirement accounts annually.

The RMD rules apply to

- Traditional IRAs
- Simplified Employee Pension (SEP) IRAs

- SIMPLE IRAs
- 401(k) plans
- 403(b) plans
- 457(b) plans
- Profit-sharing plans
- Other defined contribution plans

If your money is left in these accounts and you pass away, the Setting Every Community Up for Retirement Enhancement Act (SECURE Act)—signed into law by President Trump on December 20, 2019—eliminated the "stretch" option that allowed beneficiaries to stretch their withdrawals from their inheritance over their life expectancy with significant tax savings. The new SECURE Act now states that any beneficiaries other than the surviving spouse have to deplete the account within ten years, which, depending on your tax rate, may result in a significant tax increase.

The New SECURE Act for Beneficiaries

Eligible Designated Beneficiary

The eligible designated beneficiary would include an IRA stretch option that would apply to the spouse, persons with a chronic illness or disability, persons not more than ten years younger than the deceased IRA owner, and minor children of the decedent until they reach the age of majority (which varies from state to state). In Michigan, it's eighteen years of age for most purposes. In addition, an eligible designated beneficiary has the option to select the ten-year rule, if preferred, over the life-expectancy payments. You decide how much and when you want to withdraw the funds over the ten years.

Designated Beneficiary

The designated beneficiaries are subject to the ten-year rule if the account owner died on or after January 1, 2020. The ten-year rule also requires that IRA beneficiaries withdraw the entire balance of the IRA by December 31 of the tenth year following the account holder's death.

You can no longer take withdrawals over your life expectancy, which allows the IRS to collect more taxes in a shorter period of time. You're eligible to take your withdrawals at any time or any amount within ten years.

Non-Designated Beneficiary

The SECURE Act did not change the rules for a non-designated beneficiary (e.g., estates, charitable organizations, non-qualified trusts), but the five-year rule still applies. If a traditional owner passes away before their required beginning date (RBD), the beneficiary must withdraw funds within five years. If the owner passes away after the RBD, the beneficiary must continue withdrawals using the decedent's life expectancy.

Unfortunately, the SECURE Act wasn't passed to secure your assets; it was passed to secure more taxes for the IRS. If you reached the age of seventy-and-a-half in 2019, you should have taken your first RMD no later than April 1, 2020. If you reached the age of seventy-and-a-half in 2020 or later, you are required to take your first RMD by April 1 of the year after you reach seventy-two.

If you forget to take your RMD or don't withdraw the correct amount, you could be hit with a 50 percent penalty plus federal and state taxes. Depending on your tax bracket, you may end up walking away with only 25 percent of the money withdrawn. RMDs are required annually, so you want to avoid that mistake.

You can withdraw more than the RMD or up to 100 percent of the account value, but the taxes may be significant, and anything over the required amount cannot be credited to next year's RMD. Roth IRAs do not require withdrawals until after the death of the owner. If the assets have been established for a minimum of five years, then the RMDs can be taken tax-free. The IRS allows you sixty days to rollover or transfer your funds outside of your present retirement plan, which is a non-taxable event. If it's an individual retirement account (IRA) now, it will remain an IRA. If it's not an IRA (such as a 401(k), 403(b), 457(b), or another qualified retirement account), once the funds are transferred or rolled over, it will be classified as an IRA.

To calculate your minimum RMD withdrawal amount, use the chart below. If you're the taxpayer, you will use your age at the end of the current year, but you have to use your account balance as of December 31 of the previous year.

Required Minimum Distribution Chart for 2022

Age	Distribution period	Age	Distribution period
70	29.1	93	10.1
71	28.2	94	9.5
72	27.4	95	8.9
73	26.5	96	8.4
74	25.5	97	7.8
75	24.6	98	7.3
76	23.7	99	6.8
77	22.9	100	6.4
78	22	101	6
79	21.1	102	5.6
80	20.2	103	5.2
81	19.4	104	4.9
82	18.5	105	4.6
83	17.7	106	4.3
84	16.8	107	4.1
85	16	108	3.9
86	15.2	109	3.7
87	14.4	110	3.5
88	13.7	111	3.4
89	12.9	112	3.3
90	12.2	113	3.1
91	11.5	114	3
92	10.8	115+	>2.9

Source: www.irs.gov

Calculation Example Assuming Age Seventy-Five

Account value as of December 31 of the previous year assuming it was $500,000 divided by 24.6 = $20,325.20 for your RMD.

If you own two or more traditional IRAs, the IRS will allow you to withdraw 100 percent of your total annual RMD from just one traditional IRA, or a portion from multiple traditional IRAs to equal the total RMD owed. With multiple traditional IRAs, the IRS doesn't care which IRA it comes from as long as they get the taxes that are owed.

RMDs for employer retirement plans must be calculated separately. This includes accounts such as a 401(k), 457(b), SEP IRA, Savings Incentive Match Plan for Employees (SIMPLE) IRA, or profit-sharing account. An exception to the employer plans would be if you have multiple 403(b)s or tax-sheltered annuities (TSAs). You can withdraw the total amount owed from one 403(b) or TSA.

One hundred percent of your RMD withdrawal is taxable.

If you don't need the money, your withdrawal can be used to fund a number of things, including but not limited to the following:

- Start a grandchild's education fund
- Purchase an annuity with optional riders, lifetime income, enhanced death benefit, or long-term care
- Purchase a long-term care insurance policy
- Fund a cash value life insurance policy that can be tax-free income in retirement

You need to discuss your RMD withdrawals with a tax professional according to your personal situation to calculate the required payment for your RMDs. The IRS will make the final determination, calculations, and assessment of your RMD.

CHAPTER FIVE
Social Security Secrets

Plans are nothing; planning is everything.
—Dwight D. Eisenhower

Let's start with a little history of Social Security. Ernest Ackerman received the first check from Social Security in January 1937—a lump-sum payout of seventeen cents. Lump-sum payments were sent to people who paid into the system but retired before Social Security started monthly benefits in 1940. Ernest was a motorman from Cleveland. He retired the day after the first Social Security taxes were collected. He had contributed five cents.

Ida May Fuller was the first person to collect a monthly check from Social Security. A legal secretary who retired at age sixty-five from the state of Vermont, Ida lived to age one hundred. In those thirty-five years, she collected over $22,000. Her first check totaled $22.54.

Social Security Facts for 2022

- When you receive a paycheck, your Social Security contribution is deducted on income up to $147,000.
- Social Security deducts 6.2 percent from your paycheck, and your employer pays another 6.2 percent on your behalf (for a total of 12.4 percent).
- If you're self-employed, your contribution will be 12.4 percent.
- Forty credits are needed to be eligible to receive Social Security benefits.
- One credit is received for every $1,510 made annually.
- You can receive a maximum of four credits per year.
- The highest thirty-five years of earnings are used to determine your Social Security benefit.

- If you work less than thirty-five years, the missing years are counted as zero.
- Social Security recipients age sixty-five and younger can earn up to $19,560 before their benefit is temporarily withheld, until their full retirement age (FRA).
- In 2021, about sixty-five million Americans, or approximately one in every six US residents, received over $1 trillion in benefits.
- Among elderly Social Security recipients, 21 percent are married couples, and about 45 percent of unmarried persons rely on Social Security for 90 percent or more of their income.
- Retired workers and their dependents account for 73.2 percent of total benefits paid.
- Elderly unmarried women, including widows, get 51 percent of their total income from Social Security.

It's worth your effort to maximize your Social Security benefits so that you can minimize your future tax liability. When you decide to start your Social Security benefits, there could be a difference of hundreds of thousands of dollars for both you and your surviving spouse over your life expectancies.

When is the best time to collect Social Security benefits? There are a lot of complex strategies, rules, and regulations governing Social Security, and most people are unaware of them. If you calculate a simple breakeven for the majority of people, it will be incorrect. We recommend you become aware of all the strategies available to you.

People collecting their Social Security benefits at age sixty-two leave a lot of money on the table because they don't understand the options they have. Know what your options are before deciding what age to collect. The difference could be up to $500,000 for a single person and up to $1.5 million or more for a married couple over their life expectancy.

Think about it: This is *your* money that you and your employer contributed to the Social Security Administration for a total of 12.4 percent. If you don't want your money, they're perfectly fine with that! If you start your Social Security benefits at age sixty-two, you can't go back a year later and ask to change your benefits.

Most people don't understand their options, and they make decisions based on misinformation or on what they hear. You shouldn't be speculating about Social Security strategies, but maybe you need income out of necessity: a medical reason, unemployment, you don't think you're going to live long, or you just can't afford to use delayed retirement credits to increase your benefits later. Each person's age and how much money they'll collect can also determine how and when they decide to claim.

Don't claim your Social Security benefits unless you understand all the strategies and benefits available to you. There are strategies for people who are already collecting benefits and have not yet turned seventy, and for people who are married, single, divorced, or widowed.

Don't be fooled into thinking it's going to be easy to decide when to take your Social Security benefits. The Social Security Administration boasts 2,728 rules and guidelines outlined in a 170-plus-page booklet, with 729 options for married couples, 972 monthly age combinations, and 567 sets of calculations and strategies that include switch options. (Leave it to the government to keep it simple!)

Using strategies that are available to both you and your spouse will optimize your lifetime benefits. If you're married and both of you are entitled to benefits, a majority of you are entitled to around $1 million or more in benefits over your life expectancy. This is your money. Don't leave it with the government.

Will Your Financial Advisor Provide the Correct Advice for You to Make the Right Decisions?

Some people ask their financial advisors for Social Security advice. From our experience, most financial advisors don't have a clue about Social Security's complex strategies and guidelines. They're more interested in how your investments are going to benefit them rather than producing a Social Security optimization analysis with specific instructions to take to the Social Security Administration to increase your benefits. You should be talking to a financial professional that can assist you in this area.

Should I Ask the Social Security Administration for Advice?

Social Security representatives are actually prohibited by law to give you any personalized

Social Security advice. That includes your retirement accounts, savings, or any other money you have in order to evaluate how your decision will impact your financial future. They are not licensed financial professionals.

Social Security representatives are generally trained to focus on monthly benefit amounts for a specific person or couple, not strategies to maximize your lifetime benefits for you and your spouse (if you're married). They don't have a computer program to calculate how you can optimize your Social Security benefits. Without the computer program, it's pretty much impossible to make the best decisions. I don't see the Social Security Administration going around the country updating their computer system to pay everybody more money. That's why they won't tell you what to do; they'll ask you what you want to do.

Should I Discuss My Situation with Someone Trained in Social Security Optimization?

Absolutely. Taking your Social Security benefits at the right time will impact you for the rest of your life. It will make a difference in your lifestyle in retirement, and it will have an effect on your retirement and savings accounts. The more you collect from Social Security, the less money you have to withdraw from your nest egg.

Everyone's situation is different. That's why it's imperative to have a plan of action to coordinate the preservation and distribution of your retirement accounts to delay Social Security benefits. Taking Social Security benefits at the right time is a huge financial decision on your part, so it pays to get it right. You need to look at your options, then decide what's best for you. You have nothing to lose.

Can I Work and Still Collect Social Security Benefits?

If you decide to continue working and collect your Social Security benefits prior to your FRA, and if you're between the ages of sixty-two and the year of your FRA, one dollar of your Social Security benefit is deducted for every two dollars of earnings over $19,560 for 2022. In the year of your FRA, one dollar of your Social Security benefit is deducted for every three dollars of earnings over $51,960, which applies only to the months before your FRA.

Once you reach your FRA, you will receive the full benefit you're entitled to regardless of how much you earn. You can work as much as you want without being penalized.

How Is Social Security Taxed?

If you're a single person filing taxes in 2022 for the 2021 tax year and have a combined income of $25,000–$34,000, expect to pay income taxes on 50 percent of Social Security benefits. If your combined income is more than $34,000, expect to pay taxes on 85 percent of your Social Security benefits.

If you're a married couple filing jointly and have a combined income of $32,000–$44,000, expect to pay taxes on 50 percent of your Social Security income. If your combined income is more than $44,000, expect to pay taxes on 85 percent of your Social Security benefits.

By using tax planning, we have some clients paying zero taxes on their Social Security benefits. It's all in the tax planning. You need to know if there are strategies available to you that will increase your benefits.

How Do I Calculate Taxes on My Social Security Benefits?

Calculating taxes on your Social Security benefits can be accomplished in six steps:

Step 1: Calculate your provisional income. This involves combining half of your Social Security benefits with nearly every other source of income you have, including:

- Wages
- Pensions
- Dividends
- Capital gains
- Realized interest
- Business income
- Tax-exempt interest (such as municipal bonds)

For example, say you have $28,000 in annual Social Security benefits. Split that in half to $14,000. You've determined from the list above that you have $35,000 in other sources of taxable income. Add $14,000 and $35,000, and you have a provisional income of $49,000.

Step 2: Take the $49,000 in provisional income and subtract $32,000 (the first taxable threshold allowed for a married couple filing jointly) to get

$17,000. Multiply $17,000 by 50 percent, and you have $8,500 of taxable benefits.

Step 3: Take the $49,000 of provisional income and subtract $44,000 (the second taxable threshold for a married couple filing jointly) to get $5,000. Multiply $5,000 by 35 percent, and you have $1,750 of taxable benefits.

Step 4: Add step 2 ($8,500) and step 3 ($1,750) and you get $10,250. The result is that only 36.6 percent of the $28,000 of Social Security benefits would be taxed instead of the maximum 85 percent.

Step 5: Calculate the maximum amount of Social Security benefits that can be taxed by multiplying 85 percent by your Social Security benefits amount. So multiply 85 percent by $28,000, and you have $23,800 of taxable Social Security benefits.

Step 6: If step 4 is less than the maximum amount, then step 4 is the taxable amount. If step 4 is greater than the maximum amount, then step 5 is the taxable amount.

You'll want to manage the impact of taxes. As much as 85 percent of your Social Security benefits may be subject to income taxation.

We talked about delaying your Social Security benefits to get more money and pay less in taxes—a good reason to collect any additional money you're entitled to.

If you're married and your higher-earning spouse passes away, you would be entitled to collect 100 percent of your spouse's Social Security benefit, but you'll eliminate yours. This decreases the chances of the surviving spouse struggling financially.

Social Security will be one of the most important decisions you'll make for your retirement, and you have good reason to delay receiving Social Security benefits.

How and When Do I File for Social Security?

Our firm offers a complimentary optimization analysis for people who live in southeastern Michigan that helps you decide how and when to file for your Social Security benefits. The analysis comes with specific instructions to present to the Social Security Administration using their rules and guidelines. You'll know the exact year and month to file in order to receive the optimum payments to benefit you, your spouse, and your family.

Make sure you are aware of the strategies available to you to receive the benefits you're entitled to over your life expectancy. Your Social Security benefit is not the government's money. It isn't welfare, food stamps, Section 8 housing, or a free cell phone. It's your money that you've paid into the system for years.

Should I Delay Social Security Benefits?

There are good reasons to delay receiving Social Security benefits. Assuming your FRA is sixty-six, from age sixty-two to sixty-six, your benefits will increase an average of 6.25 percent per year. From age sixty-six to seventy, it goes into supercharged mode at 8 percent per year. That's a 57 percent increase if you delay your benefits until age seventy, plus you are entitled to a cost-of-living adjustment (COLA). In the last five years, COLA has increased 13.6 percent, and that increase continues for the rest of your life, plus any future increases (whether you delay your benefits or not).

There is no state tax in Michigan, and your Social Security benefits are not taxed as ordinary income. Social Security benefits are taxed at a lower rate and are considered provisional income. This means that working beyond age sixty-two could make a significant difference in your benefits over your lifetime.

What Else Do I Need to Consider?

Many other factors need to be considered when it comes to Social Security. You may owe federal and state taxes on your Social Security benefits, though Social Security is not taxed in the state of Michigan. To avoid paying more taxes than necessary, you need to know how to coordinate the distribution of your retirement assets, along with optimizing your Social Security benefits and using tax planning to reduce or eliminate your taxes.

Understand that every time you withdraw money, you may create a taxable event. Consider developing a plan when taking distribution from your retirement accounts. You must know your options before you file for your Social Security benefits. The goal is to provide more money for your retirement and less for the IRS. This requires a complete review of your overall financial situation to come up with strategies to reduce or eliminate your taxes.

You should also consider where to withdraw your money first: from a qualified retirement account, a non-qualified account, or a Roth IRA? Should you file for your Social Security benefit? They're all taxed differently. Taking proper distribution from your retirement assets by optimizing your Social Security, along with coordinating the withdrawal from retirement assets and tax planning will help you determine what makes sense for your particular situation.

Proposals to Fix Social Security

A couple of reasons for the Social Security dilemma are that (1) fewer workers contribute to Social Security than people who collect benefits and (2) rising life expectancies.

Our belief is that Social Security can be fixed. The following proposals have been made, but Congress moves in slow, mysterious ways:

- Raise the FRA to seventy for younger people
- Raise the earnings cap
- Change the benefits formula

- Adjust the cost-of-living formula
- Increase payroll taxes

The Social Security system will definitely change for your children and grandchildren, but if you're in your late fifties or older, you'll likely see minimal changes.

Once your Social Security benefits start, you have a sense of security that it's going to last you the rest of your life. If you have a pension (personal or company) and retirement accounts, these are valuable assets that can make a huge difference in your lifestyle during retirement. The object is to collect as much as possible from Social Security and delay your benefits as long as possible. You can always go to the local Social Security office and collect your benefits once you reach the age of sixty-two or older, and you'll be able to start receiving your benefits.

CHAPTER SIX

How Social Security Rules Affect You

It's better to look ahead and prepare than to look back and regret.

—Jackie Joyner-Kersee

In the text of Section 831 of the Bipartisan Budget Act of 2015, Social Security benefit changes were the largest since 2000 (listed as follows). They eliminated the ability to file only for a worker or a spouse benefit to all retired and spousal applicants and changed the suspension policy so that other benefits payable on the worker's record, such as a spousal benefit, are also suspended. Widowed and divorced spousal benefits were not affected.

Even with the guidelines, it may still be possible to collect hundreds of thousands of dollars more in additional benefits over your life expectancy. This makes a huge difference in retirement when you could use the extra money to maintain the standard of living you're accustomed to.

Benefits for Single People

The change was fairly simple. If you were born on or before May 1, 1950, you could have filed immediately or once you reached your FRA. Then you would have been able to maximize your benefits by delaying your Social Security benefits past your FRA and filing and suspending your benefits immediately or when you reach your FRA.

To take full advantage of the old rules, you should have maximized your benefits on or before April 30, 2016. Using the old rules to suspend your benefits would have enabled you to receive a retroactive lump-sum benefit if any changes occurred while your benefits were in suspension.

Benefits for Married People

If you're a married couple of different ages, you may have to use different rules. The specific guidelines for individuals would fall under one of three scenarios.

In the first scenario, the restricted application is still available if you were born before January 2, 1954. People born after that date do not qualify. This strategy allows you to collect benefits off your spouse. Delaying your benefits from your FRA to age seventy can increase your benefits by 32 percent.

In the second scenario, filing for your voluntary suspension will suspend the benefits of others (including your spouse and children) if you were born on or after May 2, 1950, but before January 2, 1954. Any person who has suspended benefits will not qualify for excess benefits from a spouse. These people are still eligible to file for a restricted application at their FRA or up to age seventy.

In the third scenario, if you file for voluntary suspension and were born on or after January 2, 1954, the benefits for your spouse and children will also be suspended. Persons whose benefits are suspended will not be allowed to collect their spouse's excess benefit. These people no longer have the option to file for a restricted application and receive spousal benefits.

Benefits Still Available for Divorced People

In the case of divorced couples, the rules are similar to those for married couples. You'll need to pay attention to the timelines, though. People born before January 1, 1954, will still have access to a restricted application, and those born after will not.

Many rules still apply to divorced couples. You are both still eligible to collect benefits at age sixty-two, you can both delay benefits until age seventy, and both of your FRAs stay the same. There are no changes to disability and widow benefits, and if you have already filed for benefits, nothing will change.

Whether you have filed for your Social Security benefits or not, an optimization analysis from our firm will help you determine if there's anything you can do to increase your benefits.

With 2,728 rules and guidelines to file for Social Security benefits, it can be a little overwhelming, so we've listed some frequently asked questions.

Will I Have Credits Under Social Security as a Federal Employee?

Social Security covers federal employees hired after 1983. Beginning in 1984, Social Security also began covering certain people employed by the federal government before 1983.

How Do I Determine My FRA?

Your full retirement age is decided by the year you were born. The year you were born will also determine how much your Social Security benefit will be once you start collecting benefits. See the following chart:

How to Determine Your FRA for Social Security Benefits

Year of Birth	Full Retirement Age
1937 or earlier	65
1938	65 and 2 months
1939	65 and 4 months
1940	65 and 6 months
1941	65 and 8 months
1942	65 and 10 months
1943-1954	66
1955	66 and 2 months
1956	66 and 4 months
1957	66 and 6 months
1958	66 and 8 months
1959	66 and 10 months
1960 and later	67

When Should I Start Taking Social Security Benefits?

Your benefit changes every month you wait. There are ninety-six months in which to file between the ages of sixty-two and seventy. Every month you delay increases your benefit amount.

Determining the Percentage of Your Social Security Benefits (assuming an FRA of 66)

Filing Age	Factor	Monthly Income
62	75.0%	$750
63	80.0%	$800
64	86.7%	$867
65	93.3%	$933
66	100.0%	$1,000
67	108.0%	$1,080
68	116.0%	$1,160
69	124.0%	$1,240
70	132.0%	$1,320

What is the Maximum Amount of Taxable Earnings for Social Security?

In 2022, the maximum amount of earnings on which you must pay Social Security tax is $147,000. The Social Security Administration has raised this amount in the past to keep pace with increases in average wages.

What is the Average Monthly Benefit for a Retired Worker?

The average monthly Social Security benefit expected in 2022 is $1,657. For couples, you're looking at about $2,753 monthly. The maximum Social Security benefit for a sixty-six-year-old in 2022 is $3,345. When you reach sixty-two, the amount you collect goes up every month and year until you decide to start collecting your benefits.

You can apply for Social Security retirement benefits when you are sixty-one years and nine months of age. This allows you to apply three months before you want your benefits to start.

Can I Stop my Social Security to Reapply Later to Collect More Money?

Unexpected changes may occur after you start collecting your Social Security retirement benefits. If you begin at age sixty-two and then change your mind, you can withdraw your Social Security claim and reapply at a future date. However, you must do this before you turn sixty-three, and you will also have to pay back the benefits you collected.

If you're collecting benefits between the ages of sixty-three and before your FRA, you cannot change your benefits. You may suspend your benefits when you reach your FRA and up to age seventy. You can then delay your benefits so that you can increase your benefits at a later date, and no benefits would have to be repaid.

When Can You Collect Social Security Benefits for a Child?

An unmarried child can receive benefits if they are younger than eighteen. A full-time high school student between the ages of eighteen and nineteen or a child age eighteen or older with a disability that began before age twenty-two can also receive benefits.

Will Retirees with Larger Incomes Pay More for Medicare?

Medicare will cost more for retirees with a larger income. There is no maximum earnings amount for Medicare tax, and you must pay Medicare tax on all your earnings. You can enroll for Medicare three months before your sixty-fifth birthday, and Medicare enrollment ends three months after you turn sixty-five. See the chart below:

2022 Medicare Part B Premium Costs & IRMAA
(Income-Related Monthly Adjustment Amount)

Individual tax return	Married filed jointly	Adjustment	Payment
$91K or less	$182K or less	$0	$170.10
Above $91K up to $114K	Above $182K up to $228K	$68	$238.10
Above $114K up to $142K	Above $228K up to $284K	$170.10	$340.20
Above $142K up to $170K	Above $284K up to $340K	$272.20	$442.30
Above $170K and less than $500K	Above $340K and less than $750K	$374.20	$544.30
$500K or more	$750K or more	$408.20	$578.30

Source: Centers for Medicare & Medicaid Services

Part B Deductible and Coinsurance

In 2022, your Part B deductible is $233. After you meet your deductible for the year, you typically pay 20 percent of the Medicare-approved amount for the following situations: most doctor services (including most doctor services while a hospital inpatient), outpatient therapy, and durable medical equipment.

If you are receiving Social Security benefits, the Medicare Part B premiums will be deducted from your monthly benefit. If you are not receiving Social Security benefits, you will pay the Part B premiums quarterly directly to Social Security.

CHAPTER SEVEN
Free Social Security Optimization

An investment in knowledge always pays the best interest.

—Benjamin Franklin

Optimizing your Social Security benefits is one of the most important decisions you'll make for your retirement. That's why we offer a complimentary Social Security optimization analysis for residents in southeastern Michigan. Once I discovered how much retirement money I was leaving on the table, I asked myself, "Why doesn't everyone know this?"

Since 2007, our firm has been on a mission to educate the public. We offer complimentary educational classes, or you can visit our Seminars on Call at SSRU.org. They cover numerous topics including Social Security and Tax-Free Retirement, along with FREE brief five-minute videos and eBooks.

We developed a comprehensive written action plan for your retirement assets using Social Security optimization analyses and tax-forward planning to reduce or eliminate your taxes as close to zero as possible. We're proud of the fact that we have instructed people on how to put millions of dollars into their pockets.

We enjoy what we do because we help retirement-age people eliminate their major concern: outliving their money. We're committed to assisting you on how to acquire assets using a safe-money alternative with a portion of your portfolio to provide a lifetime of income for you and your spouse.

Our strategy underestimates what you have and overestimates your needs in retirement. With our help, you'll be able to navigate your unique financial challenges, understand your money, and safely protect your assets. We're determined to give you the vital information you need to protect your hard-earned money and make a truly informed decision.

If you're like most people, you've worked all your life to establish a career, put a roof over your head, and raise your family. Market losses in or near your retirement years can be difficult to recover from and may jeopardize that hard work, all the more so if you're already retired with no income from an employer. Acquiring assets could be a game changer.

You don't want to be in a situation where there's a market correction, you no longer have a paycheck, and you're withdrawing money from your retirement accounts to cover your living expenses. Your money can disappear quickly—with disastrous effects. Instead of funding your retirement, you're depleting the funds you set aside for your retirement.

Everyone hopes to accumulate enough assets to retire. If you haven't, you will have to either continue to work and delay your anticipated retirement or retire with less money, stay home with your TV remote, and hope your money lasts as long as you do. When you retire, you don't want to worry about going back to work to support your lifestyle. If you work during retirement, you want to do it because you enjoy doing it, not because you have to.

We can help you systematically withdraw money from your retirement funds to eliminate taxes as much as possible and put more money in your pocket, not the IRS's. How your taxes are calculated will not be the same for all your assets, whether they are retirement account(s), pre-tax or after-tax retirement account(s), pensions, short-term or long-term capital gains, dividends, Social Security, or Roth IRAs (which are tax-free).

We're here to educate you on your specific situation so you can use the IRS rules to your advantage. Don't leave this to chance; timing is everything. Taxes aren't going down any time soon. What's your plan? Where do you begin?

The majority of CPAs, accountants, and tax software programs are unable to offer the critical advice you need on important tax strategies to reduce your taxes. We have a lawyer on our team with a doctoral degree and a master's in taxation. When CPAs and accountants have a tax issue, this is who they go to for advice. Our lawyer has helped many of our clients reduce or eliminate their taxes. It's not about how much you make—it's how much you keep!

Our Commitment to Our Clients

If you've acquired enough assets for retirement, our goal is to help you plan for a successful retirement. We want you to know how and when to systematically coordinate conversions to tax-free money, rollover or transfer a portion of your assets to the preservation stage for safety, and, finally, move on to the distribution stage for a lifetime of income guaranteed and insured along with tax planning.

You should be paying the minimum taxes legally possible so that your money will last throughout your retirement. Why pay more taxes than you need to?

At our firm, our clients always come first. That work will be based on your age, time horizon, liquidity needs, retirement goals, and risk tolerance. We create lasting relationships by helping people build their financial future so that they can continue to live in the way they're accustomed to in retirement. If there's any doubt in your mind that you're not doing what's right for you, or you're not doing as well as you would like and you're feeling uneasy about your present or upcoming retirement, you need to consult with a financial professional who will take your financial success as seriously as you do.

CHAPTER EIGHT

It May Be Possible to Avoid Hundreds of Thousands of Dollars in Taxes

By failing to prepare, you are preparing to fail.

—Benjamin Franklin

Taxes are a huge part of planning for retirement and are the one thing that could decimate your retirement dreams. Losing 30–40 percent of your retirement savings to taxes is probably not the kind of retirement you want. We often find tax strategies that your accountant or financial advisor may not know about. By implementing tax-forward planning, we're able to reduce or eliminate our clients' taxes as close to zero as possible.

Advisors will talk about the proper allocation of their clients' investable assets, but many won't talk about the proper allocation of investable assets to reduce taxes. We believe that it's not how much you make, it's how much you keep. The time to do tax planning is now. Take advantage of lower taxes and the tax strategies that are available to you. We can provide you with valuable insight that will carry you throughout your lifetime.

We think you'd agree with us that taxes aren't going down any time soon. Whether you think taxes are going up or not, visit the US Debt Clock website, USDebtClock.org, for a real eye-opener. There you'll see how fast the United States debt is growing in real time. As of January 2022, the official debt of the United States was approximately $30 trillion ($30,004,017,489,912). That's not billions—it's trillions of dollars, with a T, and growing. In a few years, you'll wish taxes were at the level they are today.

The IRS already has a plan for your retirement accounts. Based on your tax returns or audits, they have a good idea how much money you're going to pay in taxes. Using unlawful means to reduce your taxes is tax evasion, but there are a couple of things you can do legally. You can use the IRS's rules, when possible, to reduce or eliminate your taxes, and you can use an experienced tax professional for guidance in tax-forward planning.

Generally speaking, both the federal and state governments can tax your pension, retirement accounts, Social Security, capital gains, or dividends. When it's time to start taking a distribution from your nest egg, what's your plan to avoid paying more in taxes than you should? Look at the chart below for an example of the impact taxes can have on your pre-taxed qualified accounts.

Potential Tax Impact[*]

Current Pre-Taxed Qualified Account $834,622

The values below show two scenarios:

1. The total taxes paid if you live to age ninety, assuming you continue to keep your qualified account, take RMDs when required, and reinvest these RMDs in a taxable account.

2. The total taxes paid if you live to age ninety, assuming you roll over your qualified account to a Roth or Roth alternative account today.

Without Tax Planning		**With Tax Planning**	
Total taxes paid on RMDs at time of withdrawals	$338,126	Taxes paid on Roth or Roth alternative conversion(s)	$202,179
Total taxes paid on reinvested RMDs	$119,137	Taxes paid on account growth after conversion(s)	ZERO
Total taxes paid on remaining account value at death	$399,097	Taxes paid on remaining account value at death	ZERO
TAXES PAID	$856,360		$202,179
TAX SAVINGS			$654,181

*These materials are for informational purposes only and are not intended to provide tax, accounting, or investment advice. Be sure to consult a qualified professional about your individual situation. This hypothetical example does not consider every product or feature of tax-deferred accounts, Roth or Roth alternative account(s), and is for illustrative purposes only. It should not be deemed a representation of past or future results and is no *guarantee of return or future performance. Your tax bracket may be lower or higher in retirement, unlike this hypothetical example. The RMD calculation data is gathered from Stonewood Financial RMD calculation software based on IRS guidelines and tables and is hypothetical only. Your actual RMDs are determined by a variety of factors.*

Assuming that Trump's tax reduction goes away on January 1, 2026, you need to do something sooner rather than later to take advantage of lower taxes and avoid excessive taxation with conversion strategies you may not be aware of.

Taxes

The 401(k) has been around for forty years, and it seemed like a great idea at the time. Replace the pension, take control of your retirement, and pay taxes later. Baby boomers are now using those 401(k)s for retirement, and the pay-taxes-later concept has become a big issue. Baby boomers are finding that their retirement income may be raising their Medicare premiums, along with an increase in their Social Security tax.

The problem is people in or near retirement need tax planning. We have a lawyer with a doctoral degree and a master's in taxation who can help people reduce or eliminate their taxes over their twenty to thirty years in retirement with tax-forward planning. Most accountants or CPAs will only ask you about exemptions and reductions from last year—that is not tax planning.

You don't want to end up with a ticking tax bomb. It's perfectly legal and morally ethical to make use of the IRS rules that allow you to reduce your tax liability. You can reduce or eliminate taxable income on the following:

- RMDs
- Capital gains
- Dividends
- Ordinary income
- Social Security
- Medicare (decrease premiums)

You were probably taught ways to accumulate retirement assets to defer your tax liability. We can show you the most tax-efficient methods to spend the assets that you've acquired. Improper allocation of your investments could potentially change your lifestyle in retirement. That money is subject to taxation. What's your plan? Your objective should be to provide more money for your retirement and less for Uncle Sam.

Your retirement accounts, such as an IRA, 401(k), 403(b), 457(b), or other qualified retirement accounts, may trigger a taxable event if any taxes are owed. The IRS will want their share. You'll probably be taxed on any withdrawal from your retirement accounts, the exception being a Roth IRA. Once the account has been established for five years, and you've reached the age of fifty-nine-and-a-half, and depending on the law in the state you live in, you may owe state taxes in addition to federal taxes on your pension. Know the rules of your state. In the state of Michigan, you're required to pay taxes on your pension, so it's in your best interest to take advantage of tax breaks.

Your investments can have less importance than the type of account you use for your retirement savings. The tax advantages of qualified retirement accounts should be part of your retirement plan. Your earnings will be able to compound and grow, tax-deferred. In addition, your principal payments can be tax deductible for the year in which you contributed.

When you enter the distribution phase of your retirement accounts, what's your plan? Should you take your company pension or the lump sum and start your own personal pension? Do you collect your Social Security now or later?

In most cases, you can improve your situation if you know the correct time to take distribution from your retirement accounts. We help our clients understand the distribution phase of their retirement to minimize their tax liability to the IRS.

Retirement planning is crucial. One mistake could change your whole standard of living in retirement. Investment mistakes made while you're retired can also be devastating. You don't want to be counting your pennies during retirement. To avoid retirement planning mistakes, consult with a tax or financial professional to get it right the first time. Once you retire, you may not have a second chance.

CHAPTER NINE
Mistakes to Avoid if You're In or Near Retirement

We have some control over when we retire. However, we have very little control over how long we live.

—Gordon H. Smith, Senator from Oregon

If you are in or near retirement, about to change employment, or have left an employer, you should be looking at the option of rolling over or transferring a portion of your retirement account(s). It's very important for you to be aware that IRAs and employer retirement plans have their own distribution rules.

Employees, even after years of contributing to a retirement plan, still don't understand the fees, rules, tax consequences, or options available to them until it's too late. Use the IRS rules and tax strategies to avoid common, costly mistakes. To learn more, go to IRS.gov and type IRS publication 590-A into the search box.

We offer a complimentary, comprehensive action plan for retirement as a way to obtain valuable information that could prevent you from making costly mistakes. We review the rules and regulations with you so that you are aware of your options. We then offer recommendations on how to avoid common mistakes and pitfalls. Now that you have the information you need to make an informed decision, we make sure to address all your concerns and questions. It is imperative that you have a good understanding of your retirement assets, along with specific recommendations and an action plan. You must coordinate the distribution of your pre-taxed qualified accounts, after-taxed non-qualified accounts, Roth IRAs, and Social Security to avoid costly mistakes and put more money in your pocket.

The majority of people we meet with have been busy putting a roof over their heads, building their careers, sending their kids to college, paying for weddings, and so forth. We prepare comprehensive written plans for retirement for people so they can retire with confidence for themselves and their loved ones.

If you were on a road trip and didn't have a GPS or MapQuest, reaching your destination would be pretty difficult. Don't make this kind of mistake with your retirement. Instead, ask yourself some basic questions:

- What do you plan to do when you retire?
- What do you need to do now to secure your retirement?
- What is your desired retirement age?
- How much will your monthly expenses be in retirement?
- How much will you need for health care costs?
- How much of your retirement savings will you lose in taxes?

Once you have your answers, define your attitude toward investment risk. Know your risk tolerance and adjust your investments to where you're comfortable with the risk versus reward.

If you're in your fifties or sixties, you probably have assets set aside for your retirement. Now you should be in preservation mode to protect your assets with the conservative investments that you've accumulated. You cannot afford to lose money or make a mistake with your hard-earned retirement money.

It's easy to have an aggressive attitude toward investing when you're in your thirties or forties, and you have time and employment income on your side. When you're younger and accumulating assets for retirement, you can afford to take on more risk with your assets because you have decades to recover from any major losses.

If you don't enjoy what you do for a living, it makes working difficult. Over 50 percent of us don't enjoy what we're doing. While early retirement is a great alternative to working, make sure that you consider all the factors that are involved.

We recommend talking to a financial professional who will come up with a plan for your retirement, but in the meantime, here are a few common early retirement mistakes that you'll want to avoid.

Not Considering Health Care Costs

The number of employers covering retirees' health care in retirement is few and far between. You'll be able to collect Medicare when you're sixty-five, but it won't cover all your medical expenses. Premiums are going up, and Medicare refuses to cover some medical services. If you're traveling out of the country, you'll have various out-of-pocket costs, such as monthly premiums, supplemental insurance premiums, prescription drug coverage, coinsurance, copayments, yearly deductibles, and health care coverage.

Medigap doesn't cover long-term care, dental care, vision care, hearing aids, eyeglasses, or private-duty nursing, and many plans don't cover prescription drugs. You'll need to plan for any medical expenses that Medicare doesn't cover.

Don't assume you're going to remain healthy until the day you die. If you retire before age sixty-five, you won't be eligible for Medicare, so we recommend getting estimates for health insurance. You'll probably be shocked at the cost. Estimating your life expectancy and any medical issues makes it difficult to predict your medical costs, especially when you don't know what those costs will be in the future or when you'll need the coverage the most. Medical costs and insurance continue to rise. Before COVID-19, Medicare Part A may face insolvency by 2026, depending on what reports you read.

Not Having Enough Income to Support Your Lifestyle in Retirement

It's more important to generate guaranteed income for your retirement than to take a risk in the market with your retirement savings that you set aside for your retirement at a time when you'll need the money the most. You should be reducing your exposure in equities—stocks, bonds, mutual funds, and so forth—so that you can preserve what you have and not run out of money in retirement.

The day you retire, you may want to start collecting your Social Security benefits. In addition, if you were lucky enough to have a company pension or start your own personal pension, you can start collecting that too. It's up to you to create any additional funds, because if you don't fund your retirement, all you're doing is depleting the funds you set aside for your retirement.

It's important that you plan safely for yourself and your loved ones. No one wants to run out of money in retirement. Are you concerned about market declines or having enough money to support your retirement? If the answer is yes, then looking at safer alternatives for your money with market-type returns is an excellent way to diversify your portfolio. You'll be able to maintain your lifestyle in retirement, enjoy peace of mind, and receive a guaranteed stream of income you cannot outlive.

Not Considering Inflation

You need to consider how inflation will impact your life during retirement. If you don't, it can have a serious effect on your standard of living in retirement. If you plan on having enough retirement assets to live to a certain age in today's dollars, you're going to outlive your money.

Most financial professionals would have a plan to include about 3 percent to compensate for inflation every year. This can have a dramatic impact on how far your retirement dollars will go. Sit down with a financial professional and discuss the impact of inflation on the income you will need in retirement.

Not Considering Major Health Issues

According to Lorie Konish, CNBC personal finance reporter, "Two-thirds of people who file for bankruptcy cite medical issues as a key contributor to their financial downfall."[2] That's six out of every ten people, so it's an important part of your long-term plan to consider how much of a financial impact a major health issue or the need for long-term care could have on your retirement assets.

Insurance companies selling long-term care insurance have been reduced significantly. In the 1990s, over one hundred companies were selling policies. Now, according to our research, only about twelve companies are selling long-term care policies. To protect your assets, you

---

2   Lorie Konish, "This Is the Real Reason Most Americans File for Bankruptcy," CNBC.com, February 11, 2019, https://www.cnbc.com/2019/02/11/this-is-the-real-reason-most-americans-file-for-bankruptcy.html.

may want to consider long-term care insurance, but be aware that it may be expensive, depending on your age and health.

For an affordable alternative, many insurance companies offer long-term care to help with health care costs through life insurance or annuities. They may cover some or all of your expenses, depending on the amount of the policy. Having something is better than nothing, and the costs are reasonable.

Not Using Your In-Service Withdrawal

If you have a retirement plan where you work, you may be able to withdraw a portion or all your funds while you are still employed. There may be some restrictions, such as vesting or not having reached the age of fifty-nine-and-a-half. If you leave an employer or have retired, you can move 100 percent of your funds if you're fully vested.

Protecting the assets you have is not just important, it's common sense. We recommend moving a portion or all your assets from your employer's retirement plan to safe-money alternatives. Your employer's retirement plans will have limited options and hidden fees that you may not be aware of.

If you're concerned about losing your retirement nest egg in the market and want to avoid market corrections with your IRA, 401(k), 403(b), 457(b), or other qualified retirement accounts, the IRS allows you sixty days to rollover or transfer your funds outside of your present retirement plan, which is a non-taxable event. Just make sure you follow the IRS guidelines. If it's an IRA now, it would remain an IRA. If it's not an IRA once the funds are transferred or rolled over, it would be classified as an IRA.

Paying Unnecessary Fees

Many employees with employer-sponsored plans like a 401(k), 403(b), 457(b), or other qualified retirement accounts don't know how to find out how much their fees are, and most assume the fees are minimal. Ted Siedle, who was employed by the FCC Investment Management Division and won the largest whistle-blower award in Securities and Exchange Commission history, shed some light on pension fees in a 2019 InvestmentNews article. Siedle said, "The last 15 years, fees paid by public funds have gone up dramatically—by ten times. When I first went into Rhode Island, the pension was disclosing fees of $7 million a year. I told them they were wrong, and within a year they started disclosing fees of $70 million a year. Private-equity and alternative investment managers got greedy and went around the country and systematically eviscerated the public records laws in every state, every county, every city. There's now legal precedent for alternative investments to not have to disclose to the public their contracts, their investments, their fees, their performance."[3]

Professor Burton G. Malkiel, PhD, has spent most of his career investigating fees on investments. He is the Chemical Bank chairman's professor emeritus of economics, a senior economist at Princeton University, and the author of the classic best-selling book *A Random Walk Down*

---

3   Greg Iacurci, "Whistle-Blower Ted Siedle Sees Pensions as Hotbed for Fraud," InvestmentNews. Crain Communications, Inc., May 10, 2019, https://www.investmentnews.com/whistle-blower-ted-siedle-sees-pensions-as-hotbed-for-fraud-79481.

Wall Street. According to Malkiel, "Just 2% in fees could eliminate half of your savings."[4]

If your employer has a 401(k) plan that charges 2 percent (including hidden fees), and you worked there for fifteen years, 30 percent of your hard-earned retirement assets are gone. Thirty years is 60 percent. The point is that fees matter. They can make a big difference in how much money you'll have to retire.

Administration Fees

Administration fees generally cost anywhere from 0.2–0.4 percent. These fees help pay for the expenses to provide your statements, customer service, answering clients' questions, ensuring the plan follows regulatory guidelines, processing transactions, and keeping records.

Asset Management Fees

Financial advisors charge around 1–1.5 percent for assets under management, though that fee is reduced if the account is $1 million or more. They oversee different aspects of the

---

4 Burton Gordon Malkiel, *A Random Walk Down Wall Street: The Time-Tested Strategy for Successful Investing*, New York: W.W. Norton & Company, 2020.

fund's assets, researching investment options, and other employees handling the fund's investments.

12b-1 Fees

The minimum fee that is charged for a 12b-1 is 0.25 percent to a maximum of 1 percent of your average net assets. This includes advertising, brochures, and informational material, as well as keeping clients and potential clients informed. More mutual funds are combining a number of other costs within the 12b-1 fees, including rebates to 401(k) recordkeepers who bundle mutual funds into a 401(k) plan to sell to employees and then keep the records for their employees in the 401(k) plans.

Trading Fees

A fund incurs trading fees when buying and selling securities such as stocks, bonds, and so forth that make up a mutual fund's underlining investments. Every mutual fund will pay a commission to a securities broker each time it buys and sells a security. Then it will lose a small amount of money on bid-ask spreads that represent the difference between the actual buy and sell price of the security at the market value.

When the fund wants to sell a security, in most cases it will sell slightly lower than the market value or slightly higher when buying. When a mutual fund sells large blocks of a security, it is usually done at a lower price, which increases costs. These fees can vary from year to year, depending on a couple of things: the frequency the fund managers buy and sell the securities within the mutual fund and the number of shares the mutual fund bought and sold for that year.

Wrap Fees

Your advisor can charge you wrap fees on the value of your account, though wrap fees may vary by the dollar amount of the account, depending on the broker dealer and the investments being wrapped. Accounts with a smaller value will be charged more than an account with a larger value.

Advisors won't tell you that they can wrap around assets that are already paying fees. A mutual fund may have fees to manage the fund, and then wrap fees are wrapped around the value of the mutual fund. If you're the investor, you may be getting charged twice. Extra fees could have a huge impact on your retirement portfolio. The important thing is to be aware of what your costs are. Your investments should have nothing to do with your loyalty or personal relationship with your advisor. This is business, and you're dealing with your retirement savings, not theirs.

Revenue Sharing

Revenue sharing is the practice of padding a mutual fund's expense ratio with a general plan administration, marketing, and other non-investment-related fees, and the investor who invested in those funds pays those fees. This is where an in-service withdrawal, discussed earlier, can save you thousands of dollars in fees by having a financial professional convert your retirement savings from your 401(k), 403(b), 457(b), or other retirement plans to avoid excessive fees.

Most people we talk to are unaware of hidden charges that could cost more than the advisor's fee. Investors in mutual funds are usually paying their advisor an annual fee to invest in equities. The total cost with the additional fees could reach 3–5 percent. The costs for managing your mutual funds could result in a poor return on your investments, meaning less money for you.

Investing in Variable Annuities

Variable annuities are issued through insurance companies. They in turn invest your money in stocks, bonds, and money market instruments with up to fifty different funds that are called subaccounts, similar to mutual funds. We don't recommend variable annuities with any portion of your assets that are not insured or guaranteed, and you can lose money from the volatility of the market. As you know, past performance does not guarantee future results.

From our experience, fees with variable annuities can be excessive. The fees may include mortality (death benefit), basic expenses, administration costs, subaccount investments, account rebalancing, income riders, and annual fees. Why go through an insurance company if you want to invest in mutual funds? Just go buy no-load or low-load mutual funds and avoid the excessive fees.

Fixed-Indexed Annuities versus Variable Annuities

Consider a $100,000 fixed indexed annuity with a lifetime income rider you cannot outlive, with an average fee of 1 percent, with no loss of principal due to market volatility. Now consider a $100,000 variable annuity where your subaccount is not guaranteed from losses, is uninsurable, and has an average fee of 3.5 percent. With a fixed-indexed annuity, you're already 2.5 percent ahead of the game. That adds up to an additional $12,500 in five years and $25,000 in ten years just by reducing your fees.

It may be possible to convert your existing variable annuity to a fixed or fixed-indexed annuity without any tax consequence that will save thousands of dollars in fees. The fixed-indexed annuity has an optional lifetime income rider with no loss of principal from market volatility that's guaranteed and insured. It includes a significant up-front signing bonus and is vested into your account from day one. It also adds a great annual compounded interest rate to your personal pension. I would say that's a no-brainer.

Not Maximizing Your Employer Match

It's foolish not to participate in your employer's retirement plan if they will match your contributions. This is free money. If someone offered you free money, why would you turn it down? You should be putting in at least as much as you can afford—or as much as your employer will match. Maximize your retirement to the fullest extent possible.

About 85 percent of all companies offer matching funds, but only about 50 percent of employees will take advantage. Most employees don't participate because they don't understand how it works or how it will benefit them. It does get confusing because some companies might match dollar for dollar up to a limit or only match 50 percent of your contributions with a larger limit. In any case, your retirement account has a chance of growing and compounding tax-free until you start withdrawing from your retirement funds.

Starting early can make a significant difference. If you contribute every year, you could end up with a financially secure retirement.

Thinking You Can Work as Long as You Want

Wanting to work and being able to work are two different things. It's much easier to continue working when you're thirty to fifty years old and physically fit. The older you get, the less enthusiasm you have to work, especially if your health or energy level deteriorates. Your plans for working as long as you want may not sound exciting if you're sixty to seventy years old.

Retiring and doing nothing may not be your piece of cake. Some people would rather continue working at least part-time to occupy their time, feel productive, and interact with people. If you're going to work in retirement, it's a lot easier if you want to. You don't want to have to work because you have no other choice.

Procrastinating

There will never be a convenient time to start your financially secure retirement. The best time to start is now. If you hesitate, it just makes it harder to make a commitment to plan for your retirement with a shorter time horizon. Starting sooner can only improve your lifestyle in retirement.

We find that most people will not spend enough time properly researching their available options to secure a plan for retirement. That's why it's important to have a financial professional help you with your retirement and tax planning. Hopefully, you'll only retire once, so this is not a time to make mistakes with the hard-earned money you've worked for all your life to set aside for retirement. Check out the MyBankTracker.com survey called "Study: 1 in 5 Americans Spend More Time Planning Vacations vs. Managing Their Money" by Simon Zhen.[5]

Developing a plan for retirement will go a long way and will pay off during your retirement years. Doing nothing will not provide you with a secure retirement and can only make things worse. The sooner you get started, the more time your money has to grow and compound.

---

[5] https://www.mybanktracker.com/open-data/surveys/survey-time-planning-vacations-managing-money-301436

CHAPTER TEN

Are Annuities Safe, Guaranteed, and Insured?

I may take risks in life, but I will never risk my money. I use annuities, and I never have to worry about my money.

—George Herman "Babe" Ruth Jr.

According to Joseph A. Tomlinson, FSA, CFP®, actuary, and financial planner, "History shows that annuities have traditionally been an extremely safe investment."[6] Annuities are issued by insurance companies. The insurance

---

6 Joe Tomlinson, "How Safe Are Annuities?" Advisor Perspectives.com, Advisor Perspectives, Inc., August 14, 2012, https://www.advisorperspectives.com/newsletters12/pdfs/How_Safe_are_Annuities.pdf.

department in every state has very strict rules that the insurance companies must follow for your protection. Each state issues licenses to the insurance companies and their agents writing business in each state. In order to maintain their license, the insurance company is required to have a ratio of one-to-one in reserve for every dollar deposited.

Unlike fixed or fixed-indexed annuities, variable annuities can lose money and cannot be insured or guaranteed.

State Guaranty Fund Liability Limits

The state guaranty fund liability limits are subject to change. The information below is believed to be correct at the time of this publication. Please verify the chart's accuracy by calling the phone number for your state's department of insurance listed below.

Are Annuities Safe, Guaranteed, and Insured?

State	Maximum Liability	Phone
Alabama	$300,000	(205) 879-2202
Alaska	$250,000	(907) 243-2311
Arizona	$100,000	(602) 364-3863
Arkansas	$300,000	(501) 375-9151
California	$250,000	(323) 782-0182
Colorado	$250,000	(303) 292-5022
Connecticut	$500,000	(860) 647-1054
Delaware	$250,000	(302) 456-3656
District of Columbia	$300,000	(202) 434-8771
Florida	$300,000	(904) 398-3644
Georgia	$300,000	(770) 621-9835
Hawaii	$100,000	(808) 528-5400
Idaho	$250,000	(208) 378-9510
Illinois	$250,000	(773) 714-8050
Indiana	$100,000	(317) 636-8204
Iowa	$250,000	(515) 248-5712
Kansas	$250,000	(785) 271-1199
Kentucky	$250,000	(502) 895-5915

State	Maximum Liability	Phone
Louisiana	$250,000	(225) 381-0656
Maine	$250,000	(207) 633-1090
Maryland	$300,000	(410) 998-3907
Massachusetts	$100,000	(413) 744-8483
Michigan	$250,000	(517) 339-1755
Minnesota	$250,000	(651) 407-3149
Mississippi	$100,000	(601) 981-0755
Missouri	$100,000	(573) 634-8455
Montana	$250,000	(262) 965-5761
Nebraska	$100,000	(402) 474-6900
Nevada	$100,000	(775) 329-6171
New Hampshire	$100,000	(603) 226-9114
New Jersey	$500,000	(973) 226-9114
New Mexico	$250,000	(505) 820-7355
New York	$500,000	(212) 202-4243
North Carolina	$300,000	(919) 833-6838

Are Annuities Safe, Guaranteed, and Insured?

State	Maximum Liability	Phone
North Dakota	$250,000	(701) 235-4108
Ohio	$250,000	(614) 442-6601
Oklahoma	$300,000	(405) 272-9221
Oregon	$250,000	(503) 588-1974
Pennsylvania	$300,000	(610) 975-1572
Rhode Island	$250,000	(401) 273-2921
South Carolina	$300,000	(803) 276-0271
South Dakota	$250,000	(605) 336-0177
Tennessee	$250,000	(615) 242-8758
Texas	$250,000	(512) 476-5101
Utah	$250,000	(801) 320-9955
Vermont	$250,000	(802) 229-3553
Virginia	$250,000	(804) 282-2240
Washington	$500,000	(360) 426-6744
Wisconsin	$250,000	(304) 733-6904
West Virginia	$300,000	(608) 242-9473
Wyoming	$250,000	(303) 292-5022

Two categories are not required to be part of the state guaranty fund: fraternal life insurance companies and variable annuities. Fraternal life insurance companies are nonprofit companies created to benefit the members of the fraternal organization. Some examples are the Independent Order of Foresters, the Modern Woodmen of America, and the Catholic Knights Insurance Society.

There are many things we consider when comparing fixed or fixed-indexed annuities:

- The signing bonus
- Generous interest rates for growth
- The best lifetime income payments
- Low or no annual fees
- Best single or joint guaranteed lifetime income payments
- Insurance company ratings:
  » AM Best
  » Standard & Poor's (S&P)
  » Moody's
  » Fitch
  » Weiss
  » COMDEX (a combination of rating agencies)

Make sure your advisor is searching multiple carriers that will solve your specific situation. We are not committed to any specific insurance company. Our fiduciary responsibility and commitment is to our clients, and we shop the market for the best rates possible. Fortunately, we are an independent firm able to offer multiple annuities. We thereby create flexibility and a custom fit to the specific needs of each individual.

CHAPTER ELEVEN
Annuity Myths, Pros, and Cons

Compound interest is the eighth wonder of the world. He who understands it, earns it; he who doesn't, pays it.

—Albert Einstein

When you're younger, married, and raising a family, you may need life insurance to protect your family if you die too soon. An annuity is a way of providing a lifetime income stream for you and your spouse to protect yourself from outliving your money by living longer than expected.

Complaints are an excellent way of gauging consumer satisfaction with annuities. Out of seventy-seven insurance companies and a few hundred annuity products, there have been only three confirmed complaints filed against insurance companies that sell annuities. For more information, see annuity complaint data at: https://dfr.oregon.gov/help/Documents/complaint-stats-2020/Complaint-AnnuitiesFull-2020.pdf.

So, it's important to have proper diversification in your portfolio. You should be looking at fixed or fixed-indexed annuities to generate an income in retirement with a portion of your assets.

If you are someone planning for retirement or already in retirement, you want to know that your money will last as long as you do. Assuming a retirement time horizon lasts thirty years, you'll want to have a majority of your money in safe-money alternatives for a high probability of success.

Whether you have $250,000 or $1 million in investable assets, you need to allocate your investments wisely. We recommend you use Warren Buffet's Rule of 100, discussed in

Annuity Myths, Pros, and Cons

Chapter 2, as a way of providing an optional, safer lifetime income stream that's guaranteed and insured to support you and your family in retirement.

With the purchase of the annuity, you can set up your own optional personal pension—presently paying an 8 percent signing bonus—invested immediately upon issue, plus a great annual compounded interest rate of 7 percent added to your income rider (personal pension) for a lifetime of income. The fee for your income rider is approximately 1 percent, guaranteed and insured. Your pension will be determined by the age at which you start your pension and a percentage of the lifetime income account value and will pay you until the day you die. You can start your income at any time after one year or delay it up to ten years. Your lifetime income can be paid monthly, quarterly, semiannually, or annually. The longer you wait, the higher your income will be once you start your pension. If you let your income value continue to grow for ten years, your initial premium will double in value for a lifetime of income. If you pass away, your beneficiaries will inherit any remaining cash value in the account.

The cash value, which is the initial premium you started with, is separate from the income rider and will continue to grow if the market goes up (and so does your cash value account). If the market declines, you don't lose a dime of your principal from market volatility (minus optional income rider fees). This value may continue to grow before you start your pension and even while you're collecting it. Even if your income account value runs out of money, the insurance company is obligated to pay you until the day you die. A majority of people we talk to would rather have a guaranteed stream of income than risk their money in the market.

At our firm, we believe in annuities for a portion of your retirement savings because they can guarantee the preservation of your assets in retirement. If we were to ask people if they would give up their income from their pension or Social Security, we know the answer would be a resounding *no*. But when we recommend an annuity, their first reaction would be to decline unless they understood the many benefits of an annuity. These products are rapidly increasing in sales because traditional pensions are being eliminated along with matching funds for company-sponsored retirement accounts.

Annuity Myths

If I Pass Away, the Insurance Company Keeps the Money

Your account can be set up as a single or joint payout to you and your spouse. If you set up a joint payout and you pass away, your spouse can continue collecting your lifetime payments in perpetuity. If the surviving spouse passes away, then the contract cash value left in the account value would be left to contingent beneficiaries' children, grandchildren, or others avoiding probate. If it was set up as a single payout, the primary or contingent beneficiary would inherit any contract cash value left in the account.

Fixed or Fixed-Indexed Annuities Are Bad Because They Have Fees and Costs

Fixed and fixed-indexed annuities have no fees unless you add an income rider, which is usually about 1 percent annually. Rider fees could be for lifetime income, an enhanced death benefit, or even help with long-term care. The most widely used is the income rider (personal pension). With rates much higher than your bank or credit union offer, this is where your money will compound at a much faster rate and help you achieve financial security.

Annuities Require a Large Investment

Some annuity companies allow a minimum of $5,000 to start and allow you to add as little as twenty-five dollars.

I Have Limited Access to My Funds

Insurance companies will allow you to access your funds surrender free for required minimum distributions (RMDs), a nursing home waiver, a terminal illness waiver, an optional enhanced death benefit rider, and a rider to help with health care costs that include in-home care, adult daycare, assisted living, and nursing home care.

You can also access your funds surrender free for up to 10 percent of the cash value of the account after the first year and each year thereafter.

I Already Have an IRA or a Retirement Plan at Work and Don't Want an Annuity

An annuity may have more flexibility for access to your funds and contribution limits. It's a great way to convert some or most of your nonperforming or risky retirement accounts, whether it's an IRA, 401(k), 403(b), 457(b), or any other qualified retirement accounts to a safe-money alternative and reduce your fees.

Annuity Pros

Safety

Fixed and fixed-indexed annuities cannot invest your money in risky investments, only in alternatives like investment-grade bonds. Insurance companies also deal with reinsurers, where multiple companies share the risk instead of just one. Fixed and fixed-indexed annuities are regulated by each state and backed by the state guaranty fund.

The amount of money an insurance company is required to pay into the fund is a percentage, ranging from 1 to 2 percent of the net amount of insurance it sells within any particular state. The only exclusion would be variable annuities and fraternal life insurance companies, which are not guaranteed or insured.

Death Benefit

Beneficiaries inherit the contract cash value in case of death, along with distribution options, which avoids probate.

Estate Planning

Annuities can be used to protect assets in case of long-term care or spend down. Consult with an estate planning professional to find out how it works in your state because the rules and regulations can vary depending on which state you live in.

Unlimited Contributions

A non-qualified annuity has no contribution limits and is funded with after-tax dollars from any accounts other than qualified retirement accounts. Taxes would have already been paid when you fund an annuity. When the money is withdrawn, only the gains are taxed as ordinary income.

Tax-Deferred Growth

At the end of each year, the insurance company will calculate any index interest earned, then add that to your contract cash value based on your allocation preference and the conditions of the contract. Any decline in the index's performance will not affect your contract cash value. The funds can grow tax-deferred and are not taxed until they are withdrawn, allowing your funds to compound faster.

Commissions

With fixed or fixed-indexed annuities, no commissions or fees in the sale of the policy are deducted from your principal payments to pay a financial professional.

Annuity Cons

Penalty for Early Access

Early access may trigger a 10 percent IRS penalty, whether it's an annuity or any other investments on any withdrawals prior to age fifty-nine-and-a-half.

Penalty for Early Withdrawal

If you withdraw more than 10 percent of the contract cash value, a penalty will apply and may vary depending on the company issuing the policy. The following scenarios can alleviate penalties:

- Activating your personal pension if you added the lifetime income rider
- Annuitizing the contract for income
- Taking your RMD
- Having beneficiaries inherit the contract cash value
- Accessing up to 10 percent of the contract cash value after the first anniversary date penalty free and available each year thereafter
- Using the nursing home or terminal illness waiver

CHAPTER TWELVE
Understanding Annuities

Rule number one: Never lose money. Rule number two: Never forget rule number one.

—Warren Buffet

Today's retiree is learning that there is an important place for annuities in today's retirement planning. However, it's important to choose the correct annuity for your financial situation for it to work with the rest of your retirement portfolio. Not all annuities are the same, and there are some we would not recommend.

As an independent firm, we're not limited to a handful of companies that offer annuities. We use a computer program that searches a database to compare all annuities. We're looking for preferred ratings, current bonuses offered, interest rates that could fluctuate from company to company (just like they do bank to bank), and lifetime income payment schedules.

When used correctly, an annuity can be a very effective lifetime income (personal pension) tool for retirement. If you're in a position where you don't need an income rider, you have the option to add an enhanced death benefit or long-term care rider for a small fee. You're not obligated to take any riders, and in that case there would no fees.

With all the options you have for retirement planning, it can get a little overwhelming. If you have any money set aside for retirement, it's imperative to have a retirement plan to preserve your assets, which includes tax planning. We have found that when our clients start thinking about retirement, they start worrying about whether their money is properly invested and if they have enough money to retire with and maintain their lifestyle.

With all the political and economic unrest nationally and worldwide, investing in equities or variable investments comes with the possibility of a market decline. Each investment has its own specific type of asset-class risk that could have a major effect on your retirement portfolio. This is why you should seriously consider moving a portion of the assets you've worked so hard to accumulate to a safer alternative. Diversifying your assets provides a safer alternative with no taxes due at the time of the rollover or transfer. You also get market-type returns with no loss of principal if the market declines, and you don't lose a dime of your principal from a market correction. Zero is your hero. Surely, you would agree that you'd rather keep your money than lose it. Either way, you have a winning situation and nothing to lose.

If you purchase an annuity, you're able to make a flexible or a lump-sum payment. All annuities can have a tax advantage because your earnings will accumulate tax-deferred, resulting in a faster compounded rate of growth.

Variable Annuities

Variable annuities are very flexible, and insurers can structure their plans to fit just about any individual's needs. Be aware that an equity-based variable annuity is not guaranteed or insured. You can lose money due to market declines, and the fees can be excessive.

Advisors licensed to sell securities also sell these annuities. They're offered through a prospectus and are issued by insurance companies. Listed below are the excessive fees that may be attached to variable annuities:

- Mortality
- Expense
- Administrative
- Subaccount fees (similar to mutual funds)
- Income rider
- Rebalancing fees
- Annual fees

Fees for mortality, expense, and administration will average about 1.5 percent. Subaccount fees also average around 1 percent. Add an income rider for 1 percent, and the total fees amount to 3.5 percent. You would have to have a gain of 3.5 percent every year just to break even.

With a variable annuity, the contract cash value can be fixed or variable, depending on your investments due to market volatility. The Securities and Exchange Commission classifies variable annuities as securities and regulates them accordingly. A variable equity-indexed annuity uses the returns based on the performance of a market index. Common ones are the Dow Jones Industrial Average or the S&P 500 Index. Other investment options to invest in subaccounts include stocks, bonds, and money market instruments.

The annuity can offer a stream of income that can be paid out over a specific number of years or for the life of the owner(s).

Immediate Annuities

Immediate annuities can be purchased with a single lump-sum payment, and in exchange, they pay a guaranteed income that usually starts within thirty days.

An annuitant (person receiving payment) can elect to receive a specific payment amount for a set period of years, also known as a "period certain," which is usually five, ten, fifteen, or twenty years. If the annuitant should pass away before the end of that period, the designated beneficiary would receive the balance of payments. A "life-only option" can also be chosen, which provides payments to the annuitant until he or she passes away.

Single Premium Deferred Annuities

A single premium deferred annuity is purchased with a lump-sum payment and grows tax-deferred. If it's a qualified retirement account, 100 percent of the withdrawals may be taxable. Withdrawals from a non-qualified account may be taxable but only on gains over and above any initial premium or on any additional premiums added to the same policy (referred to as the cost basis), which is the after-tax money contributed to the annuity.

Flexible Premium Deferred Annuity

A flexible premium deferred annuity is an annuity that will accept a series of flexible payments with a variety of withdrawal options. If you choose to contribute once your initial payment is paid, then any additional payments are made at your convenience. The growth of the annuity is determined by the performance of an index such as the S&P 500 or a fixed rate of return that will not fall below a minimum guarantee.

Fixed Annuities

Fixed annuities offer fixed interest rates with a higher rate of return than CDs or high-yield savings accounts at your local bank or credit union. The fixed rate of return will not fall below the minimum rate.

Fixed-Indexed Annuities

Fixed-indexed annuities offer both the fixed option (same as above) and an index option. For the index option, earnings are linked to a percentage of the increase in an index, the most popular being the S&P 500. The percentage is the same as the participation rate, which will vary from company to company. If the index increases in value, so does the cash value. If the index declines in value, the principal is guaranteed; you won't lose any value due to market declines, and any gains will be locked in annually.

Conclusion

Taxes are a huge part of planning for retirement. Losing 30–40 percent of your retirement savings to taxes is probably not the kind of retirement you would expect. Many times, we find tax strategies that your accountant or financial advisor may not know about. By implementing tax-forward planning, we're able to reduce or eliminate your taxes as close to zero as possible. Advisors will talk about the proper allocation of their clients' investable assets, but they won't talk about the proper allocation of investable assets to reduce their taxes by hundreds of thousands of dollars in excessive taxation.

We believe that "it's not how much you make, it's how much you keep." The time to do tax planning is now to take advantage of lower taxes and strategies that are available to you. Trump's tax reduction will likely go away on January 1, 2026, which is why you need to do something sooner rather than later to take advantage of lower taxes. We provide our clients with valuable insight to carry them throughout their retirement. With a federal deficit of $30 trillion, do you think taxes won't go up?

It's essential to provide a safer income for life for you and your spouse that will establish a worry-free, financially secure retirement that can last as long as you and your spouse live. Establish your own personal pension. Insurance companies issue these annuity policies with an optional income rider guaranteed and insured.

Avoid retirement planning mistakes and take advantage of Social Security strategies to optimize your benefits. It's essential to coordinate the distribution of your Social Security, retirement assets, company, or personal pension to minimize your tax liability. Know how and when to take distribution of your assets so you can prevent paying more taxes than necessary.

Filing at the wrong time makes it possible to lose up to 50 percent of your Social Security benefits. Know what strategy to use. Don't file until you know your options—should you file now or later? For many people, Social Security is the largest and most mismanaged asset they have. Nearly three-quarters of Americans receive reduced benefits.

Social Security sounds easy, but with 2,728 rules and guidelines in the Social Security Administration manual, it's virtually impossible to figure out how and when to maximize your benefits if you don't have a computer program. This is why over $10 billion in benefits go unclaimed every year. This may be the money you're entitled to. Why leave your money with the government?

Once you're in or near retirement, improper allocation of your investments could potentially devastate your retirement dreams. Time will not be on your side. You need to think about preserving your retirement. How is your money allocated? Even if you're a conservative investor, there are no guarantees if you're invested in the market. Maybe you'll make money, maybe you won't.

To properly allocate your money, we define two categories to apply to the Rule of 100. There's what we call *guaranteed money* (safer money) and *maybe money* (money at risk). How much of your retirement money is safe? In retirement, you need three things: income, safety, and growth.

Guaranteed money will give you all three.

Instead of the traditional pension plan, you may be offered a retirement plan from your present employer, such as a 401(k), 403(b), 457(b), or other qualified retirement plans where the employee is assuming all of the risk. Market volatility can be a major concern with your retirement assets with no guarantees. There are safer alternatives to build a retirement portfolio instead of investing in traditional equities such as stocks, bonds, and mutual funds.

In a bull market (market trending up), there are safer alternatives to consider that would have the ability to participate in market-type gains. In a bear market (market trending down), you would not lose a dime of your principal due to market volatility. Fixed or fixed-indexed annuities are safe alternatives for a portion of your retirement money.

If we could show you a way that would guarantee you and your spouse an optional lifetime of income in perpetuity, would that interest you? We're not talking about some crazy scheme that has a lot of risk associated with it. We're talking about purchasing a safer investment alternative so your money will last as long as you do.

Glossary

401(k): A tax-qualified, defined contribution pension account explained in subsection 401(k) of the Internal Revenue Code. Any retirement savings contributions are provided by the employee and optional contributions from the employer, which are then deducted from the employee's paycheck prior to taxation. That money is then tax-deferred until withdrawn.

403(b): A tax-advantaged retirement savings plan available for public education organizations, some nonprofit employees, cooperative hospital service organizations, and self-employed ministers. It has tax treatment similar to a 401(k) plan. Employee contributions into a 403(b) plan are deducted from the employee's paycheck prior to taxation and is tax-deferred until withdrawn. A 403(b) plan can also be referred to as a tax-sheltered annuity (TSA), although since 1974 they are no longer restricted to annuities, and employees can also invest in mutual funds.

annuitant: An individual who is entitled to collect regular payments from an annuity. The annuitant can be the contract holder or another person.

annuitize: A set period of time during which you will receive payments from an annuity.

annuity: A contract that provides for a series of payments to be made or received at regular intervals. An annuity may be immediate, starting as soon as the premium has been paid, or it may be deferred, starting at a designated later date. Annuities are commonly used to fund a retirement.

assets under management (AUM): The total value of money or securities a financial institution manages for individuals.

certificates of deposit (CD): A promissory note usually issued by a bank or credit union with a low rate of interest for a specified period of time. You are restricted from withdrawing its funds on demand. You are able to withdraw funds, but there will be an early withdrawal penalty.

compound interest: The addition of interest to the principal, or in other words, interest on interest.

death benefit: A payout to the beneficiary of a life insurance policy or annuity when the insured or annuitant dies.

full retirement age (FRA): The age when you are entitled to 100 percent of your Social Security benefits, which are determined by your thirty-five-year work history.

Individual Retirement Account (IRA): An individual retirement plan offered by many financial institutions that provides tax advantages for a retirement savings plan and is a type of individual retirement account described in IRS Publication 590. It is tax-deferred until withdrawn.

life-only option: The insurance company pays you an income for the rest of your life but will not make payments to anyone else after you die. This option will have the greatest income possible.

non-qualified annuities: Contracts purchased with after-tax dollars that are tax-deferred until you withdraw the funds. You are taxed only on the gains, not the original investment (cost basis) that you have already paid taxes on.

qualified annuities: Purchased with pre-tax dollars, money from an IRA, 401(k), 403(b), 457(b), or other qualified retirement accounts to fund the annuity. A qualified annuity provides deferral of taxes.

required minimum distribution (RMD): The amount of money you are required to withdraw from any qualified retirement accounts. You can take your RMDs in the year you turn seventy-two, depending on your date of birth, but you are required to start your RMDs no later than April 1 following the year you reach seventy-two and each year thereafter.

rollover or transfer: A rollover is when you move assets from two different accounts, such as a 401(k) to a traditional IRA. A transfer is when you move assets from accounts that are the same, such as traditional IRA to traditional IRA.

Roth IRA: A Roth individual retirement account allows distributions that may be tax-exempt.

Individuals may make nondeductible contributions into a Roth IRA if certain income requirements are met. Qualified distributions from a Roth IRA are tax-free once the account has been established for five years. A Roth IRA offers tax-free income, including gains added to the account value for the owner and any beneficiaries.

Rule of 72: Divide seventy-two by the interest rate that will equal the number of years it would take you to double your money. For example, seventy-two divided by 6 percent equals twelve, the number of years to double your money.

Simplified Employee Pension (SEP) IRA: A retirement plan established by employers, including self-employed individuals. The SEP is an IRA-based plan to which employees or employers can make tax-deductible contributions that grow tax-deferred for employees, including the owner of the business. The employer's contributions are tax-deductible and can be made to an employee's plan, as determined by the employer.

Standard & Poor's 500: The most common index used by fixed, fixed-indexed, and variable annuities. Commonly called the S&P 500, this American stock-market index is based on the market capitalizations of the five hundred largest companies having common stock listed on the NYSE or the NASDAQ.

surrender fee: The amount charged for withdrawing money or terminating an annuity contract prior to the surrender period. Surrender charges are typically a percentage of the total premium deposited, and the charge decreases to zero over time as the annuity gets closer to the date of maturity.

surrender period: The amount of time you must wait until you can withdraw funds from an annuity without paying a penalty (surrender fee).

tax-deferred annuities: No taxes are owed on your annuity until you start withdrawals. For non-qualified annuities, only the gains are taxed. With qualified retirement accounts, 100 percent of the account is subject to taxation but only on the amount you are withdrawing.

tax-sheltered annuity (TSA): A tax-sheltered annuity allows an employee to make contributions from his or her income into a retirement plan. The contributions are a tax-deductible event from an employee's income and are not taxed until withdrawn. The employer can make direct

Glossary

contributions to the plan, which benefits the employee.

Thrift Savings Plan (TSP): A defined contribution plan for United States civil service employees and retirees and members of the uniformed services. The thrift savings plan is one of three components of the Federal Employees Retirement System; the other two are the Basic Benefit Plan and Social Security.

variable annuity: A contract created by insurance companies that allows you to invest your money within an investment portfolio, called subaccounts, similar to mutual funds. This allows you to establish a stream of lifetime income for a period of time. Unlike other annuities, a variable annuity cannot be insured or guaranteed.

About the Authors

CEO and Chairman, Senior Financial Center, Inc.

Charles Bartman is a recognized financial professional, gifted writer, and established public speaker. Charles co-authored the Amazon #1 international best-selling book *Uncle Sam's Retirement Plan* and has published articles in *Forbes*, *Money Magazine*, *CNN Money*, and numerous other media outlets. He has also appeared on Jane Pauley's CBS *Sunday Morning* show as a host of his *Sunday Morning Money Report*, has been featured on the radio with his *Monday Morning Report*, and has hosted his own radio show, *Safer Income for Life*.

Charles's dedication and commitment have enabled him to guide his clients to achieve their retirement goals. He focuses on using downside market protection for retirement income planning, reducing excessive fees, maximizing Social Security to collect more money, and employing tax-forward planning to reduce taxes to get his clients as close to zero as possible. Advisors will talk about the proper allocation of clients' assets, but many don't discuss the proper allocation of investable assets to reduce taxes by hundreds of thousands of dollars.

Charles believes that it's not how much you make, it's how much you keep.

President, Senior Financial Center, Inc.

David Bartman is recognized as one of the nation's leading experts on retirement strategies. His passion is to assist his clients in or near retirement to understand their money and protect their assets. He gives his clients the information they need to make truly informed decisions.

David understands the unique challenges his clients face in all aspects of their lives. He is specifically trained to assist them from the accumulation stage of their assets to the preservation stage to the distribution stage, all by avoiding excessive and unnecessary taxes. He also understands that with longer life expectancies, people are concerned that they will outlive their money. For many years, David has counseled hundreds of clients around the country and has preserved millions of dollars in retirement assets by assisting his clients in flexible investment strategies. These principles are what he has based his business on.

David's clients rely on his advice to sustain their lifestyle and build and preserve their wealth. He listens to each client's needs and values to determine what is important to them. People feel comfortable working with him because of the integrity he demonstrates when dealing with such delicate issues as one's personal finances. As a result, he has developed lifelong relationships. For David, his clients always come first, and he works tirelessly to achieve their goals.